NORTHWEST HERITAGE

THE CASCADE RANGE

BY RAY ATKESON

Edited by Archie Satterfield

Maps by Dee Molenaar

Published by Charles H. Belding
Portland, Oregon

International Standard Book Number 0-912856-01-7
Library of Congress Catalog Card Number 77-81400
Copyright© 1969 by Publisher · Charles H. Belding
Graphic Arts Center Publishing Co.
2000 N.W. Wilson · Portland, Oregon 97209 · 503/224-7777
Designer · Robert Reynolds
Printer · Graphic Arts Center
Bindery · Lincoln and Allen

Printed in The United States of America
Sixth Printing

DEDICATION
This book is dedicated to all people
who cherish and work for preservation
of natural beauty in our Northwest
heritage.

CONTENTS

ACKNOWLEDGMENT
During preparation of the text the author
referred to information contained in several
authoritative books including
ANCIENT VOLCANOES OF OREGON
by Howell Williams and a chapter by
Grant McConnell —The Cascade Range
in Roderick Peattie's book —THE CASCADES.
Harvey Manning also contributed
valuable advice and encouragement when
the book was hardly more than a dream.

Cascade Range

The Cascade Range—heart and backbone of the Pacific Northwest—reaches the entire length of Washington and Oregon and extends into British Columbia to the north and into California to the south. Gentle-sloping forested foothills and lush valleys stretch up to rugged crests dominated by towering glacier-clad volcanic cones, all creating a scenic paradise that at the same time contributes to the economy and climatic conditions of the land within sight of the range. Without the range, Oregon and Washington would not be the outstanding states they are; probably no other geographical feature has as much effect on the Pacific Northwest.

Thousands of streams flow down from this great mountain range like arteries pouring life blood into fertile farmlands. Many of the larger rivers are slowed briefly on their downward course to create hydro-electric power.

We who live and work in the Pacific Northwest are fortunate in having the Cascades in our front yard, although most of the mountains belong to the entire nation rather than exclusively the states in which they are situated. The U. S. Forest Service is guardian of most of the range. In addition, more than 1,700 square miles are preserved in national parks. A small percentage of the land is privately owned or administered by the Bureau of Land Management. Indian reservations extend into other sections of the range.

The national forests are managed under a policy of multiple-use, which permits the harvesting of timber, management of grazing privileges, creation of camping facilities, trails and a vast network of roads, as well as encouragement of recreational development such as winter and summer resorts and boating facilities. Perhaps the most important service of all is fire protection.

Within this vast heritage of natural beauty are a dozen wilderness and primitive areas—hundreds of thousands of acres penetrated only by trails and protected against all forms of commercial encroachment except mining developments. It is my hope that visionary actions by all who are interested in the Cascades will result in further protection of the natural beauty of these mountains and that many thousands of acres of additional wilderness areas will be added to that which already has been designated for preservation for the enjoyment of present and future generations.

Crater Lake, Lassen and Mt. Rainier National Parks are comparatively small islands of outstanding beauty administered with a combination of recreational development and preservation of natural beauty by the Department of Interior. The 700,000 acres of North Cascades National Park and Recreational Area is bringing a new, more liberal concept of recreational management. Most of the new developments and plans for the future are in the Ross Lake and Lake Chelan Recreation Areas, which serve both as buffer zones and access routes to the larger North Cascades National Park where the wilderness concept will be preserved, but with additional and improved trail systems.

The tremendous increase of automobile travel has taxed the capacity of currently available camping and picnic facilities in the older parks. Numerous trails within park boundaries have, in some cases, virtually become paved or hard-packed walks in over-used areas that no longer can serve the purpose for which they were originally designed.

The logical answer is continuous expansion to meet the ever-increasing requirements for the varied recreational resources, including the more remote areas not yet accessible. Preservation and expansion of dwindling wild areas is a very real problem that will not be easily solved. The new North Cascades National Park and Recreation Area is a giant step in the right direction.

The Cascade Range is high enough to create a barrier over which only the most severe storms from the Pacific can lift their loads of moisture to reach the semi-arid regions of Eastern Oregon and Washington. Upon reaching the mountains, they are forced to leave an abundance of moisture along the west slopes of the range, which accounts for the dense forests and lush undergrowth common to that area. In the winter, storms are more general and persistent in their invasion of the Northwest coast. The higher slopes and crests of the range accumulate an extremely deep blanket of snow, and more moisture escapes over the top than in the summer, moving on to other lesser mountain ranges and the plains of the wheat and cattle country.

Thus a vast natural storage of moisture is held in the form of well-packed snow and full reservoirs to be released into streams, irrigation canals and power projects that are the envy of the rest of the nation. These natural resources, too, should not be abused indiscriminately.

The range was a major barrier to be hurdled by pioneers and a formidable obstacle to travel between Eastern and Western Washington and Oregon until recent years, but it now has been conquered and tamed by numerous easy-grade highways across relatively low-elevation passes. In most cases, the passes are kept open the year round by fleets of giant rotary plows despite deep winter snow on the high slopes.

The Cascades, so varied in character, also vary a great deal in width. The Columbia River, in a display of nature's wisdom and practicality, found one of the most narrow spots of the range to carve its way through to the Sea. Now, travelers by rail or highway can speed, in less than an hour, through the entire width of the Cascades on the level water grade routes paralleling the mighty river. It doesn't take much longer—but with some added elevation— to cross from the lowlands and cities of Puget Sound over Snoqualmie Pass to the semi-arid climate east of the mountains. Other routes are longer and slower, but what once was considered an ordeal, and in some cases virtually impossible, has become a pleasure for Northwesterners who can change their climate or landscape to suit their particular desires by a relatively short and extremely scenic trip across the mountains from anywhere east or west of the Cascades.

This is a mountain range incomparable for its effect on the lives of the people and the character of the land that borders it. It is, indeed, the Northwest Heritage.

Rugged Mt. Shuksan stands guard inside the western boundary of North Cascades National Park. Picture Lake in the foreground is in Mt. Baker National Forest.

Flower-sprinkled meadows on Miners Ridge unfurl
toward vast panoramas of snow-crested mountain
peaks and forested valleys in the Glacier Peak
Wilderness.

Glaciers blanket the mountains as far as the eye
can see in Glacier Peak Wilderness. The LeConte
rolls down the foreground slope; at left, the Chicka-
min clings to the steep north side of Dome Peak,
and Glacier Peak dominates the distant skyline.

Autumn gold of Larch trees glow in beautiful contrast among evergreen conifers on the eastern slope of the range.

Aspen reach in regal splendor from a hillside in
Okanogan National Forest where large groves color
the mountain slopes in the autumn season.

Summer flowers mingle with colorful rocks in Glacier Basin in the historic Monte Cristo mining region. North Cascades of Washington.

Small pine trees cling stubbornly to the sparse soil of a tiny lava island in a crystal-clear lake on the crest of Oregon's Cascades.

The high slopes of the Cascades are blessed with abundant snowfall which assures many months of winter pleasure for thousands of skiers. Numerous winter resorts take full advantage of the varied terrain from northern California through Oregon and Washington to British Columbia.

The realm of St. Nicholas on the crest of the Cascade Range where Christmas trees by the million sparkle in winter sunshine after each new snowfall.

A fantastic ice grotto beneath Paradise Glacier
becomes a kaleidoscope of color as sunlight filters
through the scalloped walls and lofty ceiling to
blend with the light of a flare.

Lake Cavanaugh mirrors the birth of a new day as serrated crests of the North Cascades are silhouetted by delicately tinted clouds.

A shallow pool gathers a random collection of
autumn foliage from vine maple, dogwood and
cottonwood trees.

Wild rhododendron bloom profusely in many areas
along the western slope to the crest of the range.

Rainfall in the western foothills is so abundant that
maple groves in some areas wear the mossy raiment
associated with rain forests.

Indian summer tranquility in Eagle Creek Canyon
not far from the Columbia River Gorge.

Creation

The creation of the Cascade Range is a story of violence and turbulence stretching back over millions of years, beginning long before man arrived on this continent.

In the beginning most of Oregon and Washington lay beneath the sea; then periods of violent unrest within the earth produced an unstable foundation as upheavals, fractures and eruptions began occurring on the bottom of the sea. About 50 or 60 million years ago the forces from within became so violent that the ocean floor burst through the surface of the sea, forming new land. Through fissures in this land, molten lava poured forth and flowed from the higher ridges back into the sea again. The ridge was not high, and after this first period of unrest and expansion, there followed a long period of comparative inward peace and stability.

The sea relentlessly pounded and tore at the new shoreline. Erosion of time and the elements reduced the new land to a plain, only slightly above the pounding surf.

Perhaps 10 million years passed, then pressures within the earth built up again to such an extent that the new land was subjected to even more violent upheavals, and the volcanic action transformed the flat plain into a ridge, the real beginning of the range.

Changes in geology of the Northwest was not confined to the ridge that eventually was to become the Cascade Range. To the west, the earth crust beneath the sea buckled and heaved until it rose to form a long, low peninsula extending for hundreds of miles north and south paralleling but farther west than our present coastline. An inland gulf was temporarily trapped between this peninsula and the Cascade ridge. Later, the land subsided beneath the ocean surface again, only to eventually rise to create our present mainland.

To the east, tremendous lava flows reached southward creating the Columbia River lava plateau, which is thousands of feet deep in places and extends across most of Eastern Washington. Violent volcanic activity created cones and mountains in the area that now is Eastern Oregon. Marshlands and lakes developed in lowlands between these mountains. A mild, humid, semi-tropical climate prevailed in the Northwest during that time and fossils found recently show that where there was land, forests of tropical vegetation flourished in the lower elevations and redwoods on the higher slopes. Animals unlike any now on earth roamed the forests. As more time elapsed—periods so long that man cannot comprehend — the volcanoes continued to erupt; land subsided and rose again, and erosion proceeded at a rapid rate.

The Middle Miocene Period of 15 to 20 million years saw the volcanic activity increase far more violently and continuously than during any previous period. This range, which had graduated to mountainous proportions, experienced eruptions of lava from fissures rather than from cones, and this stage of activity continued to pile lava and fragmental materials higher and higher and spread them out over the range. The climax was a general uplift of the entire range of a fantastic magnitude.

This continuous volcanism and uplifts would have created a towering range had it not been for successive sinkings of the lava crests due to their own terrific weight and constant undermining activity. But it was not until the end of the Miocene Age that the range finally became so high that climatic conditions were affected. There now was a barrier standing solidly in the path of moisture-laden winds from the Pacific. The lush semi-tropical vegetation and the redwood forests disappeared east of the mountains for lack of moisture and the western slopes accumulated more moisture than before, and there vegetation flourished.

There followed still another period of formation when the so-called shield volcanoes rose above the range. All these millions of years while the mountains rose, streams became torrents roaring down the slopes, tearing and eroding deep canyons. And during this time the climate gradually became colder.

Now, in its last stage of growth that began perhaps a million years ago, even more spectacular volcanic activity began with explosive eruptions that created our great conical volcanoes reaching thousands of feet above the rest of the range.

In Oregon, these lofty peaks rose along the eastern side of the older range, and in Washington, Mt. Adams also grew on the east side of the high divide. Farther north, Mt. Rainier, monarch of them all, chose its throne just west of the old range. Northward, Glacier Peak and Mt. Baker lifted their peaks on the western slopes of the range. Mt. St. Helens in Washington's Southern Cascades apparently was the last to be created in this conical image, and it, too, is west of the crest of the range. This phase of volcanic activity continued sporadically for hundreds of thousands of years, coinciding with development of the Ice Age.

As the climate became more frigid, all of Northern Washington was buried beneath a vast sea of ice. The entire Cascade Range even into Northern California came under the influence of Ice Age glaciers. The glaciers, powerful in their erosive characteristics, gouged and scraped along the granite crest of the North Cascades, sculpturing tremendous canyons and valleys that were not revealed until the climate changed again and the ice retreated upslope and northward.

Some of the glaciers reached many miles east and west of the mountain crest. One gouged a trough about 75 miles long and in places 300 feet below sea level, leaving in its wake a mammoth dam at its terminus that dwarfs anything man has yet created. Behind that dam the melting ice created a huge lake—Lake Chelan, more than 50 miles long—that occupies a large portion of that deep trough. Its surface is 1,096 feet above sea level and the beautiful lake reaches from the semi-arid plains of Eastern Washington to the heart of the Cascades where 8,000-foot mountains tower above the blue-green waters.

Hundreds of glaciers still are at work on the upper granite slopes of the North Cascades and on the lofty volcanic peaks such as Mt. Baker, Glacier Peak and Mt. Rainier, all of which are almost completely encased in ice above timberline.

A new cycle seems to have become established about 1950. Since then, most of the glaciers in Washington's Cascades have been advancing farther down the mountain slopes and also increasing in depth. Those in Oregon have shown little consistent change in these recent years.

Of all the volcanic activity along this fascinating range, the most terrifying was the final phase of creation and destruction of Mt. Mazama. Ashes and superheated rocks were spewed more than 100 miles from the 12,000-foot peak until all that remained was the exterior shell. Then, in a thunderous climax, Mt. Mazama collapsed, leaving a cauldron five miles in diameter, 3,000 to 4,000 feet deep with precipitous walls that now form the rim of Crater Lake, perhaps the most beautiful body of water in the world. Even as the cauldron filled with water, volcanism of a lesser magnitude continued until eventually a symmetrical cone, Wizard Island, rose several hundred feet higher than the present surface of the lake. Large, U-shaped valleys, carved by glaciers still are plainly visible where they sweep down the lower slopes of old Mt. Mazama.

The destruction of Mt. Mazama was witnessed by Indians, who by that time had arrived in the Northwest. Carbon dated artifacts found in the caves near Fort Rock far to the northeast of Mt. Mazama indicate that terrified people were there during the spectacular eruptions and the eventual self destruction of the mountain.

Each great peak of the Cascades has its own fascinating story of birth and growth as well as more recent sculpturing by the elements. Thousands of people now living witnessed many major eruptions of Mt. Lassen, the southernmost peak of the Cascade Range, which was violently active from 1914 to 1917. Minor activity continued for years after that. Mt. Rainier and Mt. St. Helens were active as recently as 1870.

The Three Sisters region in Oregon's Central Cascades is a mysterious land of lunar-like landscapes created by lava flows and eruptions. And only about a thousand years ago, a huge lava flow reached as far as the headwaters of the McKenzie River, where it became a solid dam across a deep canyon, creating Clear Lake and burying a mature forest. Many of the skeletons of that forest still are standing and are visible beneath the surface of the clear, frigid water.

As glaciers carved and sculptured, so did the countless streams; some of them finding natural passage down the slopes through earth fractures that today are spectacular landmarks. Others tore out their own courses through thousands of years of flood torrents racing down the mountains. Only two rivers, which we now know as the Columbia and the Klamath, were able to tear their way through the barrier as it continued to rise higher and higher.

In Oregon, virtually all of the early structure of the Cascades has disappeared. Vast forests cloak the lower slopes which rise only slightly more than 5,000 feet to the crest. It is the more recently created volcanic cones, large and small, that dominate the character of this section of the range as well as most of the Southern Cascades of Washington. From Mt. Rainier northward, only two great volcanoes—Glacier Peak and Mt. Baker—tower above the vast land of high granite mountains, deep valleys and canyons.

It has taken more than 50 million years of unrest, violence, erosion and radical climatic changes to create the Cascade Range. And what a masterpiece of beauty it is!

In the last stage of creation a long period of explosive volcanic eruptions built up lofty conical peaks that reached high into the clouds above the rest of the Cascade Range.

The Ice Age still exists in the high mountains of the Glacier Peak Wilderness where large glaciers, such as the South Cascade, continue their sculpturing action.

Glaciation has left deep bowls on the lofty plateaus of the Stuart Range; here, the beautiful Enchantment Lakes have filled these depressions to overflowing.

Lake Chelan partially fills a huge glacier carved
valley which reaches 50 miles from the heart of the
North Cascades to the Columbia River in the plains
of Eastern Washington.

Granite slopes show dramatic evidence of ancient
glacial action.

A 20th Century holocaust, created by forest fires, recreates conditions in the Cascades as they might have been witnessed hundreds of thousands of years ago when the volcanic cones spewed lava, ashes and smoke during the painful growth of the range.

Crater Lake half fills the gigantic cauldron left by
the collapse of Mt. Mazama about 6500 years ago.
Rain and melting snow keep pace with seepage,
stabilizing the surface level at nearly the same
point, although there is no visible outlet to the lake.

Volcanic activities of various periods are revealed in this air view of an outcropping of lava, known as Rock Mesa, which flowed and cooled beside LaConte Crater in the Sisters Wilderness.

Spectacular flows of Obsidian from fissures at the base of the South Sister terminate at Devils Lake on the Cascades Lakes Highway. This is one of the most recent products of volcanic activity in Oregon's Cascades.

The highest Crater Lake in the Cascades has a brief view of daylight late in the summer when ice melts on top of the South Sister.

Below and to the right are several small lakes in the Chambers cluster. Each of these colorful pools are held in pockets created by glacial moraines.

The Klickitat Glacier still carves its great circ on the east side of Mt. Adams. Little Mt. Adams, a parasitic volcanic cone, rises to the left from the Ridge of Wonders in the Mt. Adams Wilderness.

Streams flowing down the mountain slopes sometimes find a line of least resistance through ancient
faults or fractures, as has Oneonta Creek, flowing
through Oneonta Gorge.

The Eagle Creek Punch Bowl has been sculptured
by flow and swirl of the stream, creating a masterpiece of beauty.

Southern Cascades

The Cascade Range assumes its identity in the vicinity of Mt. Lassen National Park and joins the northern extremities of the Sierra Nevadas near the Feather River. Mt. Lassen was the last of the Cascade volcanoes to show activity with nearly 300 eruptions of varied intensity occurring between 1914 and 1921. Though the peak has shown little evidence of new volcanic eruption, there are areas in the surrounding park of great interest to visitors because of past and present thermal activity.

Shasta Dam on the Sacramento River has created a huge lake where waters of the Sacramento and Pit Rivers have been backed up into tributary valleys and canyons to create a scenic 365-mile shoreline. Intended primarily for reclamation and power purposes, Shasta Lake is becoming increasingly popular for boating and other water sports.

Farther north, Mt. Shasta rears its double-coned summit 14,162 feet above sea level to dominate all of Northern California, and missed being the highest peak in the Cascades by less than 300 feet. It long has been the hub of timber industry and is familiar to interstate travelers because it towers directly above a mainline railroad and Interstate Highway 5.

Mt. Shasta so dominates Northern California that beauty spots such as Castle Crags State Park and the Sacramento River Canyon above the lake are overlooked by many travelers speeding through the area. Virtually no one today is aware that one of the most intriguing combinations of springs and waterfalls of the Cascades, aptly named Mossbrae Falls, sprays from the canyon walls of the Sacramento near Dunsmuir, and both highway and railway pass within a few feet of a huge spring that is the headwaters of the Sacramento River at Mt. Shasta City. The lure of this great mountain is enhanced by a fine highway up its slopes to give access to the Mt. Shasta Ski Bowl at the 8,000-foot timberline.

From almost any place within 50 to 100 miles east or west of the entire length of the Cascade Range there is at least one volcanic peak, as exemplified by Mt. Shasta, that overshadows the lesser ridges along the crest. In Southern Oregon it is Mt. McLoughlin. This symmetrical cone, although only 9,495 feet, thrusts high above lakes, valleys and surrounding forests. It is not well known except by Oregonians and is something of a pleasant surprise to new visitors to the Northwest when they see it either from the Rogue River Valley to the west or Klamath Lake to the east. During the eight or nine months of the year it is capped with snow, it is one of the Cascades' most strikingly beautiful peaks. Not far south of Mt. McLoughlin is the 23,000 acre Mountain Lakes Wilderness.

Crater Lake, the jewel of the Cascades and considered one of the "Seven Wonders of the World," is the heart of Crater Lake National Park. It is such an outstanding attraction that numerous other scenic and geological wonders of the area are seldom seen by most park visitors. Were they located elsewhere, these beauty spots would be principal attractions. For example, not far from the lake, the famous Rogue River barely gets under way from its source before its rampaging waters suddenly funnel underground and out of sight into a lava tube, seemingly too small to swallow it; then, about a hundred yards farther down the forested mountain slope, it gushes out again to roar through a deep, narrow gorge and continue its race toward the Pacific.

No author, photographer or artist can ever capture the full beauty and geological wonders of Crater Lake when it is viewed under favorable conditions. Too many park visitors drive to the rim, look and leave unimpressed. Sometimes this is due to unfavorable atmospheric conditions. I recall my first visit to the lake on a normal summer day. I was one of those who failed to see what all the shouting was about. Intangible elements were lacking to set the mood for full enjoyment of this great natural wonder. Since then I have learned that one should spend many days around Crater Lake to fully enjoy its great beauty and changing moods. The Rim Road, encircling the lake, provides opportunities to study it from numerous viewpoints. A hike down the trail to the water's edge and a boat ride around the lake on a calm, clear morning are experiences long to be remembered.

As in most National Parks, there are many animals and birds that seem to enjoy park visitors as much as the visitors enjoy them.

The highway is open all year for the pleasure of off-season travelers. Those who have the good fortune to reach the lake rim on a clear day following a winter blizzard, I am sure will agree that this is one of the world's most beautiful sights. I must stress "the fortunate ones" because during winter months, such ideal conditions are rare. Clouds and storm conditions are more the rule than an exception at the 7,000 to 8,000-foot rim and a great deal of snow falls during the winter. Giant rotary plows carve deep canyons in the snow to keep the highway open to the rim.

Fine highways, forest roads, and trails interlace the crest and slopes of the Cascades. From Crater Lake's North Rim Road, a grand panorama lures the traveler to Diamond Lake nestled in the forest between the challenging spire of Mt. Thielson and the snow-crowned dome of Mt. Bailey. Most Oregon fishermen contend that this five-mile-long lake is the greatest in all the Northwest. Early-season weekends emphasize the overwhelming agreement on that score. Oregon's largest campground parallels almost the entire east and south shores of Diamond Lake, but latecomers often look for more distant camps because of overcrowding. Even the fish may have trouble maneuvering among the boats that spread over the surface of the lake on weekends.

A few miles from Diamond Lake down the Umpqua River Highway is a unique waterfall near the headwaters of the Clearwater River which tumbles through a bower of vivid green moss that in places completely blankets the cascading water. Below the falls, the stream flows more leisurely through a small forest campground. It is only one of hundreds of waterfalls in the range, no two alike, and none should be missed, although it would take a lifetime to see them all.

Mt. Thielson and Diamond Lake.

A deep, clear, rock-bound pool in the North Umpqua River sparkles beneath early-morning sunlight
in the forested foothills.

Clear Water River Falls pours over a small cliff to
be swallowed by a deep blanket of green moss near
the headwaters of the stream on the crest of the
mountains. Only a small portion of the falls is
shown in this view.

Snow-draped timberline trees on the rim of Crater Lake stand regally above the colorful waters of the lake.

A winter fairyland is created in Crater Lake National Park where Ponderosa pine contrast beautifully with a new blanket of snow.

The snow-crowned dome of Mt. Bailey looks down on forest-bound Diamond Lake, one of the most popular lakes in the Northwest with fishermen and campers.

Early-morning sunlight glistens across the deep
blue waters of Crater Lake.

Mt. Shasta, the 14,162-foot monarch of Northern
California, reflects the Alpen-glow of a winter sunset as its lower slopes are shrouded in shadows
toward the end of day.

The lofty double volcanic cones of Mt. Shasta reach high into sunset-tinted springtime clouds floating across volcanic buttes and sagebrush lowlands north of the mountain.

One or more of the spectacular volcanic peaks of the Cascade Range can be seen from many places either west or east of the mountains. Here Mt. McLoughlin, Oregon, though not as high as most of the major peaks, dominates the skyline from Klamath Lake on the east.

Mt. Lassen, California is never more impressive
than after the first autumn snowfall. It is especially
beautiful when viewed across Manzanita Lake.

Twin falls are joined by a hundred or more springs that pour from the moss-covered lava cliffs to create one of Northern California's most scenic attractions in McArthur-Burney Falls State Park.

Oregon's Central Cascades

A fantastic land of volcanic creation, some of it so rugged that it resembles the moon's surface, dominates the vast forests, lakes and streams of Oregon's Central Cascades. In the heart of this region is woven a variety of scenic beauty, lava fields, cinder cones, sportsmen's paradise and towering glacier-clad peaks unlike anything else to be found on this continent.

A large portion of this mountainous region is accessible by several fine all-year cross-state highways. The 100-mile Cascade Lakes Highway and improved forest roads penetrate the Central Cascades. Countless lakes know the sound of motorboats; others are restricted to rowboats, canoes and sailboats. Some of the Cascades' finest campgrounds nestle in the forest surrounding many of these lakes and rivers; summer homes and resorts line the shores of a few. To round out the attraction of the area, winter sports developments are located at Willamette and Santiam Passes, and skiers enjoy some of the west's finest slopes and snow conditions on Mt. Bachelor.

In the heart of this mountain paradise is the Sisters Wilderness encompassing the Three Sisters and Broken Top Mountains and several other lesser peaks, lava flows, cinder cones, sylvan lakes and dashing streams. Nearly 200,000 acres of natural beauty is preserved here, the second largest wilderness area in Oregon. There are many well-used trails interlacing the forests and lakes; other trails lead to routes that reach to the glaciers and summits of higher peaks.

Forest-bound Diamond Peak dominates still another wilderness area of 35,440 acres overlooking Odell and Crescent Lakes, which border the wilderness and form a center of recreation near Willamette Pass. Other valuable areas being preserved much as nature created them are those with Mt. Washington and Mt. Jefferson as their apex. Jefferson Park, a hanging alpine garden at the foot of Mt. Jefferson, is so beautiful that it has become almost too popular. Trails to several lakes and streams attract countless hikers, fishermen, campers and mountaineers. Mt. Jefferson is one of the most challenging and picturesque peaks in the Northwest. It is unfortunate that Jefferson Park is such an overwhelming magnet for outdoor lovers because there are countless other areas in and near the Mt. Jefferson Wilderness that defy description of their scenic beauty. Hunts Cove, south of the mountain, is a comparatively unknown alpine parkland. Many lakes nestle in picturesque rocky pockets and dense forests between Olallie Butte and Park Ridge, some within easy walking distance from motor camping areas at Olallie and Breitenbush Lakes. Many of these beautiful lakes are in the Warm Springs Indian Reservation.

The ponderosa pine forest of the Metolius River area is popular for summer homes, camping and fishing, dude ranches and other resort facilities. The clear, cold Metolius is born as a full-grown mountain river in a huge spring at the foot of Black Butte, a high, symmetrical, forest-covered volcanic cone. Other springs and streams of equal volume rush to join the Metolius in parklike meadows a few miles downstream.

The McKenzie Pass Highway, first of the present-day Cascade pass routes, in many ways is one of the most spectacular. Those who surveyed the route seem to have chosen the most difficult terrain they could find, and in locating it they carved directly through one of the largest lava flows in the state to reveal to travelers landscapes that might have been transplanted from the surface of the moon. Grand panoramas encompassing the Three Sisters, Mt. Washington, Three Fingered Jack, Mt. Jefferson and other peaks are unfurled from the lava fields on the crest. However, the pass is open only in the summer months.

Other more recent and natural routes that are open all year are the North and South Santiam Highways. The latter is joined to the McKenzie Highway at Belknap Springs by a modern, easy-grade route that swings the motorist within a few hundred feet of Sahalie and Koosah Falls. These thundering cataracts rank with the best in the Cascades for beauty. The three highways eventually become one to continue across the crest and down the eastern slope of the range.

The hundreds of lakes and streams in the Central Cascades help make this an outdoor paradise unexcelled anywhere in the Northwest. Actually I would be remiss to compare any specific region of the range with another because each area boasts its own individuality, each incomparable in its own way.

A fantasy of winter sculpturing on the timbered crest of Oregon's Central Cascades.

Wild currant and trillium are thrilling harbingers
of spring after the long winter months end their
seige on the western foothills and valleys.

The Three Sisters and other volcanic snow caps of the Cascades dominate the western skyline of Central Oregon.

The Metolius is born in frigid springs among pines as a full-fledged river and flows toward the snow-crowned cone of Mt. Jefferson on the distant sky-line.

The clear blue waters of the upper McKenzie boil
and swirl in effervescent beauty as the stream
rushes down the forested mountain slopes.

Not far from its birthplace in the Cascades, the
McKenzie thunders over a lava cliff at Sahalie Falls
and rushes on through the forest.

Roaring Creek lives up to it's name as it rushes down a steep timber corridor of moss covered stones.

In the cool depths of a virgin forest Breitenbush
Gorge engulfs the swift flowing waters of Oregon's
Breitenbush River.

Beautiful Green Lakes lure many hikers into the
heart of the Three Sisters Wilderness.

Vine maple fringes a colorful pool in the solitude
of an evergreen forest so dense that only filtered
sunlight penetrates to tint the foliage in pastel
shades of autumn.

Jefferson Park is a hanging alpine garden of wild-
flower sprinkled meadows and picturesque lakes
in the Mt. Jefferson Wilderness.

Decks of cloud caps reach thousands of feet above the craggy summit of Mt. Jefferson. Condensation of moist air currents frequently result in cloud caps that hover over high mountains.

The colorful volcanic spire of Mt. Washington towering above talus and wilderness forests flaunts a challenge to mountaineers. The challenge is repeated by Three Fingered Jack and Mt. Jefferson on the distant skyline.

South Silver Creek plunges nearly 200 feet from
lava cliffs to be swallowed in the shadowed depths
of the forests in the Silver Falls State Park, where
autumn has decorated vine maple foliage.

Spire-like evergreens thrust skyward from a picturesque island that appears to float on the waters
of Sparks Lake at the foot of the South Sister.

Guardians
Of The
Columbia

Three great volcanic cones of the Cascade Range have been linked together by Indian legend and modern romanticism. Mt. St. Helens and Mt. Adams in Washington and Mt. Hood in Oregon were the subject of a legendary triangle that has no parallel in history. Modern interpretations vary to some extent. Louitt (Mt. St. Helens), the maiden, was courted by Klickitat (Mt. Adams) and Wy'east (Mt. Hood) until the affair finally erupted into a battle such as the world has never since seen. The battle was so furious that during the action the "Bridge of the Gods" which spanned the mighty Columbia River Gorge was destroyed, leaving only a vast area of forest-covered debris and small lakes to suggest the possible geological evidence of such a tremendous bridge. Wy'east was left alone in what now is northern Oregon; Klickitat and Louitt remained in the area now known as the Southern Washington Cascades.

So much for legend. Each of the great peaks could easily be the subject of its own book. And so could the Columbia Gorge that cleaves the center of the Cascade Range so that the great river can flow on to its rendezvous with the Pacific.

Mt. Hood is the dominant peak in the vast Mt. Hood National Forest. Pioneers bent on reaching the fertile valley of the Willamette River in Western Oregon followed the almost impassable Barlow Trail through these forests, skirting the southern base of the mountain. Others fought their way down the Columbia River to the same destinations. In passing, those hardy people viewed the grandeur of Mt. Hood with understandable awe, and some pioneers estimated its height at 18,000 feet.

An Englishman, William Broughton, was the first white man to report existence of the mountain. He sighted Mt. Hood from his ship a hundred miles down the Columbia, which appeared to flow directly from the great snow-covered peak.

We now know that Mt. Hood is only 11,245 feet high and gives birth to several streams, some of which flow into the Columbia making an infinitesimal contibution to the volume of the West's greatest river.

Even though the peak failed to equal those early-day estimations, it still reigns over a large piece of geography. It is the highest of all Oregon mountains, and of the three Guardians, has become by far the most familiar to the greatest number of people. Thousands have climbed its summit over many routes. Its glaciers are spectacular and some are easily accessible for exploration by experienced mountaineers. The lower slopes echo to the happy sounds of winter sports enthusiasts enjoying the complex of resort facilities around its base reached by fine all-year highways. The Mt. Hood Loop and portions of U. S. 26 easily traverse many miles of virtually the same route followed by the Pioneer Barlow Trail that produced such hazardous experiences over a century ago.

The Mt. Hood National Forest now is a patchwork pattern of clear-cut logged areas interlaced by hundreds of miles of access roads. Power transmission lines slash through the big timber at the base of the mountain carrying electrical power from the great dams that have harnessed the Columbia. Only a very small area of wilderness beauty in the vicinity of Mt. Hood has been set aside for preservation in its natural state, in addition to the vast forests of the Bull Run watershed that fills reservoirs of clear water for the Portland area. Mt. Hood and its surrounding forests, lakes and streams are being used more than most other mountain regions in the Cascades: The Mt. Hood area has succumbed to civilization.

The Columbia River Gorge, its mountainous sides lined with waterfalls and tributary canyons, has, since pioneer days, been the natural and most used gateway through the mountains. Its innumerable scenic attractions are a mecca for outdoor enthusiasts and city folk who find recreation easily accessible here. Visionary conservationists have managed to preserve a considerable amount of natural beauty along Oregon's Columbia River Highway despite the inroads of civilization. There are many trails for hikers who enjoy exploring the deep canyons and enough spectacular viewpoints to avoid overcrowding. Several fine state parks add to recreational opportunities to help preserve the beauty of the Gorge.

Mt. St. Helens is becoming familiar to more and more lowlanders. An excellent highway and many forest roads, some of which still are only rugged logging roads, reach high up the timbered slopes toward this symmetrical volcanic cone that so nearly resembles Japan's Fujiyama. Spirit Lake at its northern base is ringed by timber, and in these forests are public and youth-organization camps. Boating and other resort facilities also are available on the 12-mile shoreline, and the lake is the setting for some of the most beautiful views of the mountain. A paved highway reaches up to the timberline from Spirit Lake where visitors may further pursue their enjoyment of the mountain.

Mt. St. Helens appears to be a mild and friendly mountain; and it is, if treated with the respect it demands. However, it has seen its share of tragic accidents as have most high mountains. The ascent to the glacier-covered dome is not difficult but should be assaulted only by experienced climbers or under experienced leadership and with proper climbing equipment. This also applies to virtually every glacier-clad peak in the Cascade Range.

Mt. Adams is the least-known of the three guardian peaks. It ranks third in height and size of all mountains in the range, exceeded only by Mt. Rainier and Mt. Shasta. Mountaineers have conquered it from all sides; the most frequently climbed route is the south side as is the case with its legendary rival, Mt. Hood.

For many years a good, surfaced highway has approached Mt. Adams on the south. As timber harvest has increased, so have the number and miles of roads around it. Some of them reach to timberline; others wander in the forests far below, passing various lakes, streams and viewpoints.

The Mt. Adams Wilderness, small in size at 42,411 acres, but rugged in its beauty, is explored by few hikers. The Ridge of Wonders, for example, is not well known, yet it can be reached by a rather short, steep climb up a trailless slope through Hellroaring Canyon not far from road's end. (A trail crosses the ridge at a lower point.) The views unfurled from the rim of the ridge, which is several miles long, are among the most spectacular mountain views in the Cascades, and widely traveled mountaineers agree that the Ridge of Wonders' view is one of the greatest in the world.

Here the Klickitat Glacier tumbles steeply several thousand feet from the summit into a deep circ it has carved on the east face of the mountain. And there are other alpine areas in the Mt. Adams Wilderness that rival the views from the Ridge of Wonders.

Surprisingly, for many years a small sulfur mine was worked directly on the 12,307-foot summit of Mt. Adams. Horses packed dunnage and sulfur up and down the south slope, and a handful of hardy miners trudged up the weary miles to and from work on weekends. It is unlikely that they made any dates during the work week. Just before operation of the mine was discontinued, the miners were transported on a rather indefinite schedule to and from work in a ski-equipped plane. The extremely rich deposit of sulfur resulted from ancient volcanic action that is evidenced all around Mt. Adams in various geological phenomena such as cinder cones and lava flows. Some of these lava flows, like others in Central Oregon and near Mt. St. Helens, are honeycombed with "lava tubes" or tunnel-like caves that often extend for miles beneath the forests. One near Mt. Adams has served as a natural cold-storage warehouse for farm products; another is draped with ice stalagmites and stalactites the year around.

Mt. Adams eventually will become as well known as Mt. St. Helens and other more famous peaks in the Cascades.

Wild rhododendron in full bloom set a beautiful foreground for this view of Mt. Hood, scraping the clouds far above Lost Lake and surrounding forests.

Mt. St. Helens, one of the younger mountains in the range, has an extremely smooth, rounded and symmetrical cone that varies little when viewed from any direction. This winter scene shows the southern contour.

In keeping with the beauty and character of Mt. St. Helens, several youth camps and public campgrounds are situated around forest-bound Spirit Lake north of the peak.

Mt. Adams, third highest peak in the Cascades, is tremendous in size, and its character and contours undergo radical changes when viewed from different directions. In this scene, a picturesque forest road points toward the mountain from autumn-tinted meadows pierced by alpine fir to the northwest of the mountain.

The great east wall of Mt. Adams is dramatically revealed from a vantage point on the rim of the Ridge of Wonders in the Mt. Adams Wilderness. The Klickitat Glacier tumbles 4,000 feet into a huge circ it has carved on the face of the mountain.

Dramatic snags of a ghost forest near Mt. Hood's timberline create a striking foreground for this view of evening clouds rolling over the Cascades. Mt. Adams towers above the distant horizon.

Multnomah Falls, the most famous of numerous waterfalls in the Columbia Gorge, plunges over a 620-foot lava cliff into an autumn setting beside Oregon's Columbia River Highway.

Towering giants of a Cascade forest reach skyward above this autumn scene of vine maple and fern flourishing on the forest floor.

Winter snows linger on the majestic cone of Mt. Hood long after spring has taken over in the orchards and flower-carpeted foothills of the Hood River Valley.

The summer ushers in high adventure for mountaineers getting an early-morning start for a climb up the glaciated north face of Mt. Hood. Eliot Glacier will be traversed on the ascent route.

Alpen-glow lingers on the slopes of Mt. Hood long
after the winter sun has disappeared below the horizon.

Snow and ice sculptured timberline trees silhouetted by the rosy glow of a winter sunset.

A Christmas-tree vista of the snow-mantled cone
of Mt. Hood.

Winter storms seem to have transplanted a land of
fantasy from another world to the timberline crest
of Oregon's Cascade Range.

A peculiar quirk of nature transformed a woodland lake in the southern Washington Cascades into a mirror of death. Apparently caused by fluctuation of the water level in the lake when an outlet beneath a nearby lava flow became plugged.

The photo on the opposite page shows the same lake when it was a setting of unusual beauty as autumn decorated the foliage of stately old cottonwood monarchs.

A young stream seeks its way through a mountain meadow where a variety of wildflowers bloom in colorful profusion.

Streams
And
Lakes

The Cascade Range could well have been named for the hundreds of streams cascading down its slopes from high snowfields, glaciers and springs. Thousands of white-water rapids are created where the creeks and rivers tumble through boulder-strewn canyons, earning the right of responsibility for christening this picturesque mountain range.

Actually, when the Cascade Range was named, little if anything was known of these many cascading streams that now are so popular. Pioneers who fought their way across the deserts and mountains to reach the Oregon Country after enduring months of hardship on the overland journey, found one more great obstacle to be overcome. Here, where steep-forested mountains reach into the clouds above the Columbia River, was a great rapids—The Cascades—which, as stated earlier, the Indians believed was created by the fall of the Bridge of the Gods. The pioneers experienced such difficulty in portaging around, or rafting through the treacherous rapids that this proved to be the most hazardous obstacle in the last mountain range they had to cross to reach the fertile valleys of

the western slope. They called the place the Mountains of the Cascades, which eventually was shortened to the Cascade Range. Ironically the Cascades of the Columbia no longer exist. Many years ago they were obliterated by construction of Bonneville Dam which raised the water level far above the rapids.

No other river of the Cascade Range remotely compares with the powerful Columbia, but there are several large rivers, many small ones and thousands of streams that are born near the crest or down along the slopes of these mountains.

The Skagit is the largest of the Northern Cascade rivers. The most striking aspect of the Skagit as it flows into Puget Sound is its coloration, caused by dissolving silt from innumerable glaciers which feed into its upper reaches via smaller streams of glacial origin. The Skagit has for many years been a prime source of hydroelectric power. Diablo and Ross Lakes, created by power dams on the Skagit, will become even more popular upon completion of the new Washington Pass Highway and are incorporated into recreational aspects of the new North Cascade National Park.

The Stehekin River, flowing down the east slope of the North Cascades into the upper end of Lake Chelan, colors the waters of that beautiful lake with glacial silt for several miles. The lake is unlike any other in the world. Its climate varies from semi-arid to heavy rainfall at its two ends. Some small resorts nestled on its shore where the mountains rise precipitously 6,000 feet above the water can be reached only by boat or float plane.

Countless lakes and streams of all sizes in settings as varied as they are in number can be found on the crest and slopes of the Cascades. Some lakes are held in pockets created by terminal moraines at the end of ancient and existing glaciers; others are lost in the dense forests and seldom seen by man.

Clear-water streams, gushing from springs or lakes, are joined on their downward journey by rampaging torrents of muddy water from melting glacial ice. The Skykomish, Tye, Wenatchee and Methow are among the most familiar rivers in the Washington Cascades because they parallel highways. Equally popular are Lake Wenatchee, Fish Lake and beautiful Cooper Lake with its spectacular mountain view. These and others are popular recreation areas, and state parks, forest camps and resort facilities make many lakes more enjoyable for those who prefer their outdoor life mixed with a minimum of effort.

There still are many lakes and streams for the hardy individuals and organizations that prefer to get away from civilization. Lyman Lakes, the upper Suiattle River, Miners Creek, Bridge Creek all are familiar to hikers of the North Cascades, and there are other streams and lakes even more remote to be "discovered" by more adventurous hikers and climbers who distain the ease of trail hiking.

Rapids and waterfalls add their spectacular beauty to the Cascades. In my opinion, one of the most spectacular of the great Northwestern waterfalls is Wallace Falls, which has stirred the curiosity of all who travel the Stevens Pass Highway. Curiosity is about all it has rated through the many years it has been viewed from the comfort of automobiles because relatively few have attempted or been able to locate the six-mile round-trip trail that reaches through the timber to this beautiful falls.

Several other beautiful waterfalls, both named and unnamed, are seen only by a few people. I'll wager that some, within a few hundred yards of the principal cross-mountain highways, have been seen by no more than one per cent of the people who speed across the mountains. One of the most picturesque cataracts I have photographed roars down a rocky cliff within a hundred feet of the Stevens Pass Highway. I have spent many enjoyable hours on different occasions beside the swift-flowing Tye River at the base of the falls, and never in all my visits there—which requires a 100-foot scramble to reach it—have I seen another soul.

Another lake that should not be ignored is Lake Waptus, reached by a trail from the Cle Elum River. Its setting is as beautiful as that of Cooper Lake with the added pleasure of solitude. Not far from the Cle Elum Valley, as the crow flies, are the aptly named Enchantment Lakes, surrounded by jagged granite cliffs and spires of the Stuart Range. To reach them, one must climb a steep 12-mile trail that gains 6,000 feet in altitude from Icicle Creek, a beautiful clear-water stream that flows into the Wenatchee River near the town of Leavenworth, which has been re-modeled into a replica of a quaint Bavarian Alpine village. There probably is no cluster of lakes in the Cascades so close to civilization and at the same time so remote as the Enchantment cluster.

There are other rather large lakes beside or near the Snoqualmie Pass Highway, but they are artificial and of interest more for boating and fishing than their beauty. The Snoqualmie River tumbles down the west slope of the Cascades in two main forks, each high-lighted by cascades and waterfalls climaxed by spec-tacular Snoqualmie Falls after the forks have joined near North Bend. Although the falls have been harnessed to produce electricity, they still are quite spectacular for several months of the year.

The Chinook Pass Highway follows White River on the west and The Naches east of the pass. East of the crest the Cougar Lakes Basin is accessible by trail from Bumping Lake Campground. There also are those in Mt. Rainier National Park, such as Tip-soo Lake and Reflection Lake that are small but beau-tiful and familiar to thousands of people. To the south, the Cowlitz River, which is the water-level route for many miles of the highway across White Pass, is another of the rivers that is well on its way to becoming a chain of lakes behind power dams.

One of the most beautiful lakes in the mid-Cascades of Washington is Packwood, reached by trail and nestled in a forest setting at the foot of peaks of the Goat Rocks Wilderness with a superb view of Mt. Rainier as a reward for a bit more hiking to a vantage point.

Spirit Lake at the foot of Mt. St. Helens, which has been described elsewhere, rivals the beauty of them all. It is my hope that the virgin forests sur-rounding the lake will continue to be preserved. Other beautiful lakes have been less fortunate and their natural beauty destroyed.

Several little gems of lakes are easily reached by forest roads north of Mt. Adams. It is here that the Cispus, Klickitat and Lewis Rivers are born in alpine beauty, the latter of which has become a stairway of man-made lakes as it flows through the foothills. The smaller East Fork of the Lewis at this writing still flows free with many clear, cool swimming and fishing pools interspersed with rapids and small waterfalls.

Since the Columbia has been harnessed for hydro-electric power, small tributary streams have become increasingly important in preservation of the salmon migrations. Several hatcheries are successfully estab-lishing annual runs into the Wind River, Little White Salmon, Eagle Creek, and Tanner Creek. Most of the tributaries in the Columbia Gorge are small but spectacular in their beauty. No less than a dozen famous waterfalls result when the streams plunge over the steep mountains to reach their rendezvous with the Columbia. Others, beyond motorists' view, can be reached by popular scenic trails.

Lost Lake is by far the most beautiful in the Mt. Hood National Forest, although several others are equally popular for camping, fishing and picnicking. Nearby Bull Run Lake, which is Portland's major water supply, is virtually unknown despite its beauty in a setting of unscarred forestland. It is, however, inaccessible to the public.

Travelers will note a gradual change of character in the Cascade Range from end to end. The hundreds of rugged, glacier-covered peaks of the Northern Cas-cades give way to less rugged terrain dominated more by individual volcanic peaks farther south. Forests spread across the entire range and clusters of lakes become more frequent and extensive. Lakes, few in number in the immediate vicinity of Mt. Hood, be-come almost countless in the lake basins around Olallie Butte, Mt. Jefferson, The Three Sisters and on down to the Southern Oregon border. There is one unique little tarn near Mt. Hood that is a jewel among lakes—Little Crater Lake, or as it is more appropri-ately called, Turquoise Pool. It is a deep vertical-walled clear pool in the middle of a marshy alpine meadow south of the mountain, probably created by the collapse of a subterranean stream.

The Clackamas River drains a large area of the Cascades as it rushes down the west slope to enter the Willamette near Oregon City. Its lower reaches long have been harnessed for power but many miles still flow free. Numerous riverside campgrounds and the forest-bound highway and forest roads of the Clackamas Watershed make the area a particular favorite of sportsmen.

Oregon leads the nation in development of state parks, many of which are in the Cascades. Perhaps the most popular is Silver Falls Park in the foothills of the west slope near Silverton. Two branches of Sil-ver Creek converge here and a dozen waterfalls, vary-ing in height to nearly 200 feet, tumble down through deep-forested canyons where easy trails hug the pic-turesque streams, tunnel through canopies of vine maple growth and even traverse narrow ledges di-rectly behind shimmering curtains of falling water.

Forest roads reach into the heart of a cluster of lakes near Olallie Butte, and a hike to the top of the butte reveals a view of more than 20 lakes. Nearby Breitenbush Lake is the northern gateway to the Mt. Jefferson Wilderness, reached only by trail where more beautiful alpine lakes are located.

The Breitenbush, Santiam and Metolius are the best known streams between the Clackamas water-shed and the McKenzie. To choose a favorite lake among the many would be impossible, but one is unique among them all—Clear Lake at the headwaters of the famed McKenzie River. It was created more than a thousand years ago when a lava flow dammed a deep canyon. There are many lakes in the Cascades named Clear Lake, but none deserve the name more than this one where the crystal clarity of the water is intensified in many places by white pumice sand on the bottom. The water is frigid—about 40 degrees—due to the springs that flow constantly from lava and forests around its shoreline. The most unusual aspect of this lake is the standing ghost forests of ancient trees that reach up from the bottom where they have been preserved by the deep, cold water for more than a thousand years. It gives one an eerie feeling to float silently in a rowboat on the surface of the lake, seemingly in danger of scraping the tops of the standing trees, plainly visible beneath the surface.

The McKenzie is a full-grown and boisterous river where it flows from Clear Lake to thunder over Sahalie and Koosah Falls, just a mile downstream. Power dams are located below Koosah Falls, but the McKenzie flows free for many miles below Belkap Springs.

The Sisters Wilderness, surrounding the Three Sisters peaks, encompasses more streams and lakes than can be explored in a lifetime of vacations. The streams, born in the glaciers and meadows of the crest, are small in the wilderness but beautiful, coming in varied sizes and colors. High up in the saddle between the South and Middle Sisters, in a spectacular area of rocks and mountains void of vegetation, a cluster of colorful small glacier-fed lakes are caught in glacier moraine pockets. They are known as Chambers Lakes and each is different in color due to dissolving glacial silt. Farther down, in a lava and glacier-created alpine valley between the Sisters and Broken Top Mountain, are Green Lakes, three small alpine beauties that live up to their name.

Outside the wilderness, Scott Lake is one of another small group of popular lakes accessible from the McKenzie Pass Highway, and to the south the Cascades Lakes Highway leaves no question in the visitors mind about the reasons for its name. It loops up around several popular lakes and spur roads shoot off to others. Most popular of these are Sparks, Todd, Elk, Lava, Cultus and Waldo.

The Deschutes River, which claims Little Lava Lake as its birthplace, hardly gets under way before it is impounded by man-made dams, creating large reclamation reservoirs. Finally escaping its bounds, the Deschutes reaches a bit farther south and east to continue its journey down the mountain slopes, then turns north and is joined by the Little Deschutes to carve its way through deep canyons east of the Cascades until it is used for more power and reclamation projects before it flows on to the Columbia.

Man-made dams also trap the Willamette River, which eventually becomes the largest Cascade tributary of the Columbia as it flows northward paralleled by both a busy highway and railroad.

The North and South Forks of the Umpqua River, with their deep pools slowing the beautiful clear streams in picturesque pockets of rock between noisy rapids, make these alluring streams for fishermen or hikers. The Rogue, too, gets off to an exciting start as it tumbles down the mountains past the towering Mill Creek Falls.

Southern Oregonians who want some peace and solitude find it in the Seven Lakes Basin south of Crater Lake National Park, or another cluster of small lakes and tiny ponds in the Mountain Lakes Wilderness.

In Northern California, the Sacramento, McCloud and Pit Rivers contribute to huge Shasta Lake behind Shasta Dam. McArthur Burney Falls State Park is highlighted by the beautiful twin falls that pour over a high lava cliff, from which a series of springs pour through mossy drapes to join the falls as they thunder down into a pool at the bottom of a deep canyon.

These are some of the more exciting streams and lakes that, with the peaks, glaciers and forests, make the Cascade Range so essential to the grandeur, recreation and economy of the Pacific Northwest.

A stream is born in a bed of lush green moss on the
roof of the Cascade Range.

A young mountain stream seems to grow impatient in its race down the slope, dashing over boulders and across the mossy floor of a dense forest.

A small lake in the North Cascades appears to be awakened by the rising sun that penetrates a veil of fog.

A fisherman found solitude on the shore of one of Mt. Baker's Chain Lakes, which are reached only by a trail.

Cascade streams pass ever-changing beauty as they flow swiftly down rock-strewn corridors, then dash over cliffs into mysterious granite grottos in the North Cascades.

A couple of fishermen enjoy their sport as they
run the riffles of Oregon's McKenzie River early
on an Indian Summer morning.

Lost Lake mirrors the majestic cone of Mt. Hood
cloaked in a fresh robe of snow which reflects the
rosy glow of an early winter sunset.

The Kalama River nears maturity as it leaves the
forested foothills, as does Green River where it
flows through colorful Green River Gorge near
Puget Sound.

The rugged crags of Bonanza tower above glacial-
fed Lyman Lake in the Glacier Peak Wilderness.

Lush meadows and evergreen forests surround
Todd Lake, one of Oregon's favorite mountain
playgrounds.

Autumn colors mingle with evergreens along the
steep slopes above the White Salmon River racing
to its confluence with the Columbia.

The Skykomish has reached maturity as it leaves
the Cascades, where it was born in high snowfields.

Salmon leap high above foaming waters of a rampaging stream as they fight their way to spawning grounds in the mountains.

Wallace Falls, one of the most spectacular in the entire range is a short distance north of the Stevens Pass Highway.

The Wenatchee is a river of many moods. In places it loafs along, lingering in deep, green pools to reflect the changing seasons, then takes off to race energetically in a series of rapids through Tumwater Canyon.

The mighty Columbia is the only stream that had the power to continue its flow through the Cascade Range to the sea. All others flow down the western or eastern slopes.

The Columbia has been civilization's most serviceable stream and the most natural east-west travel route. It performs its tasks well, and despite the heavy usage much of the natural scenic beauty on the south side of the Columbia Gorge has been preserved in numerous parks by farsighted action of dedicated conservationists. Unfortunately the natural beauty of mountains along the north side of the gorge have not received equal concern for preservation.

Realm
Of A
Monarch

Mt. Rainier long has been known as the "Monarch of the Northwest" and unquestionably rules over the Central Cascades and Puget Sound region of Washington. The great glacier-crowned, volcanic dome towers 14,410 feet above sea level and more than 8,000 feet above closely surrounding mountains. It is the highest and largest peak in the entire range and is almost completely covered with snow and ice of 26 named glaciers, and is the center of the 380-square-mile Mt. Rainier National Park.

Despite the hazardous conditions on its upper slopes, Mt. Rainier is a favorite conquest for experienced mountaineers. Several hundred reach its summit each year and thousands of park visitors explore some 300 miles of trails, including the famed 90-mile-long Wonderland Trail that encircles the mountain near timberline. Magnificent scenery can be seen by driving to Paradise Valley near timberline on the south side, and Yakima Park and Chinook Pass in the eastern area of the park also are served by splendid highways. Other spur roads penetrate from the west and north.

Hundreds of beautiful alpine meadows near timberline are a riot of colorful wildflowers during the summer season; few mountain areas in the world can compare with the floral display of the national park. After the summer ends, autumn foliage perhaps even more beautiful than the summer colors takes over until winter comes.

A five-mile round-trip trail leads up gentle lower slopes to the famous Paradise Glacier Ice Caverns. Paradise is one of the smaller of the 26 glaciers, many of which come down below timberline. The Emmons on the northeast slopes is about five miles long and a mile wide, making it the mountain's largest.

Many lesser peaks, such as those in the Tatoosh Range and on Sunrise Ridge, offer magnificent views of Mt. Rainier and other parts of the Cascade Range. The Tatoosh, south of the mountain, is harshly serrated and slopes away into the valley of the Cowlitz River. Farther south, glacier and snow-covered peaks of the rugged Goat Rocks Wilderness rise above the Cascades, attracting countless outdoor recreationists each summer. Several trails, including the Cascade Crest Trail, penetrate and traverse these alpine meadows with the most popular trail climbing through the forest for about five miles to Snow Grass Flats, which is the picturesque heart of several alpine meadows with frigid springs quickly growing into mountain streams flowing down through the forests.

The Cascade Crest Trail, as it is called in Washington, traverses the wilderness. It is the major trail in the Cascades and reaches from Canada to Mexico. Oregon originally called it the Skyline Trail, and like Washington, still calls it by its original name, although the official name now is the Pacific Crest Trail. It can be explored from take-off points where it crosses highway passes or from numerous access trails throughout the range, and nearly every summer groups of students as well as other outdoor enthusiasts hike the length of either Washington or Oregon on this great trail.

The Goat Rocks, south of the Monarch, are relatively low—averaging 8,000 feet—but vary considerably in climbing difficulty. All slope moderately to the south and steeply to the north, where glaciers cling to high circs below rocky pinnacles.

Farther south, Mt. Adams and Mt. St. Helens are clearly visible on good days, and Mt. Hood in Oregon can often be seen from several vantage points around Mt. Rainier. Northward, as far as the eye can see, the Cascades stretch in rugged beauty.

In addition to the highways to Paradise Valley and Yakima Park, White Pass and Chinook Pass climb across the crest of the Cascades near the Monarch. Chinook Pass is closed by avalanches during the winter months. A popular ski area is located on White Pass and one of the finest and largest winter-sports playgrounds in the Northwest is Crystal Mountain, where highways are open the year around. The Paradise Highway also is open throughout the year, but ski facilities are minimal.

The immediate area around Mt. Rainier offers so much for the curious visitor that it is doubtful that even the park rangers themselves have seen all the Monarch's realm has to offer.

Mt. Rainier, Monarch of the Northwest, thrusts
its 14,410 foot dome high above a lei of early
morning clouds.

The serrated ridge of the Tatoosh Range reaches
toward the clouds above fields of wildflowers.

This view of Mt. Rainier and Tipsoo Lake is revealed suddenly to travelers crossing Chinook Pass from the east.

A spectacular stream pours down the alpine slope of a vast glacier circ from its birthplace in Goat Lake, which is nestled among the rugged mountains of Goat Rocks Wilderness.

Snow grass flats in Goat Rocks Wilderness is traversed by Snow Grass Creek which meanders aimlessly across the grassy, flower strewn meadows.

A mountain stream is born in a moss-bowered
spring in the Goat Rocks Wilderness.

Within a few hundred feet, other springs join its flow and it leaps exuberantly over a colorful cliff above Snow Grass Flats.

Shooting Star, or Bird Bill bloom in a mountain meadow.

A picturesque monument of past glory stands as a grim reminder of havoc that can be wrought by a forest fire.

Paradise River is only a creek as it leaps over small
cliffs, then pauses in deep pools on timberline slopes
of Mt. Rainier National Park.

A field of Avalanche Lilies replaces receding snow-fields on alpine meadows.

Spires of alpine fir thrust skyward above foliage of
blueberry and mountain ash as autumn storm
clouds gather around the great dome of Mt. Rainier.

Paradise Ice Caves, a constantly changing, multi-room palace, is sculptured by air currents beneath Paradise Glacier.

Thousands of years of sculpturing by nature's tools
has hewn the dome of the Monarch so that no two
view-points will reveal any resemblance of character. Lake Eunice, to the northwest reflects a glacier
scarred rounded dome, and a trail on Mazama
Ridge south of Mt. Rainier shows an entirely different character of massive grandeur.

Magnificent vistas are constantly unfurled from the
Goat Rocks Wilderness. One of the most familiar
is the north face of Mt. Adams standing above the
hazy horizon.

North Central Cascades

The north-central section of the Cascades is closest to the densely populated Puget Sound area as well as Central Washington's cities and the Columbia Basin. As a result, this beautiful section of the range is subjected to heavily concentrated recreational and commercial use.

Roughly speaking, the Snoqualmie and Stevens Pass Highways are the boundaries of the North Central Cascades, and the Snoqualmie Pass area is a prime example of the destructive inroads civilization can make on nature. The four-lane highway (Interstate 90) is very essential to the economy of the state, but it would be difficult to find a place where civilization's progress has found more ways to destroy outstanding natural beauty than is so evident here for several miles across the crest of the Cascades. The four-lane highway might be described as a blessing in numerous ways, one of which being that many travelers can speed through the mountains without seeing too clearly the blighted area, and, too, the highway gives access to roads and trails into the back country for those thousands among us who wish to forget civilization's problems for awhile.

During the winter, nature does its best to obliterate the scars with a beautiful blanket of deep snow which, ironically, is the direct cause of much commercial development in the area. The most ambitious complex of winter-sports facilities in the Northwest is spread across the summit around Snoqualmie Pass where thousands of winter-sports enthusiasts congregate through the winter months.

The nearness of the North Central Cascades to Washington's most densely populated area could result in the assumption that this entire mountain area is overrun with people and commercialization. Fortunately, this is not true. There is a wide variety of spectacular scenic beauty and remote wilderness solitude in a surprisingly short distance from the hum of motor traffic and commercial developments, not all of which is within the previously mentioned boundaries. Some splendid, unspoiled alpine beauty to the south of Snoqualmie Pass is penetrated only by trails, but it is to the north that the real wilderness is found.

Within a few miles hikers can lose themselves in virgin evergreen forests where lakes and cascading streams dominate the scenery. More ambitious hikers and campers can follow trails into the rugged high country where glacier-covered mountains and craggy summits overlook the wilderness of Alpine Lakes. Here, many beautiful lakes fill high, hanging glacier-carved valleys and waterfalls thunder from lake to lake as streams are born and grow on their way down the mountains.

There are many lakes in this area that even the most ardent hikers and climbers seldom explore. It is a wilderness area in the purest sense and should be officially designated as such and preserved for present and future generations; nowhere will such an area be more needed in the future than places such as this where commercialization hasn't yet reached the point of no return.

Not far from Alpine Lakes and the spectacular peaks of the Cascade divide is another wilderness stronghold of an entirely different character, but perhaps even more spectacular and remote. The Stuart Range, a spur reaching out to the east, is considered part of the Wenatchee Range of the Cascades and is unique in its isolation. Isolated geologically as an upthrust of striking granite crags many miles in length and towering alone thousands of feet above deep valleys and canyons surrounding it. Mt. Stuart dominates the range and the surrounding landscape. It is a formidable challenge to expert mountaineers who must hike a few miles before they can begin the precipitous ascent. Dominating as it is, Mt. Stuart plays scenic second fiddle to a mountain-bound paradise on the opposite, or eastern, end of Stuart Range. Enchantment Lakes, an aptly named cluster of alpine lakes, are nestled in glacier-carved pockets on a high granite plateau surrounded by towering spires, crags and small glaciers.

The lakes are reached by a long and sometimes steep trail from Icicle Creek. Despite the fascinating beauty of the Enchantment Basin, it is not crowded with campers and explorers because the area has been familiar to comparatively few hikers. But its fame is spreading rapidly.

Once the area is reached, hikers find that it is unlike any other in the Cascades. There are many granite slopes easy to climb with another lake or tarn behind nearly every little ridge. It is always a thrill to reach the northwestern edge of what is called the "Lost World Plateau" at Aasgard Pass where the mountains drop off into space. More than 2,000 feet below is Colchuk Lake, a beautifully tinted body of water that seems to defy the eye to pass on to the panorama of deep valleys and the serrated crest of the Cascades beyond.

For the advanced mountaineer, there are hundreds of challenging pinnacles and precipitous cliffs around the Enchantments and all along the rugged ramparts of the Stuart Range.

Now that much of the North Cascades has been preserved in parklands, wilderness and national recreation areas, it is my hope that more attention will be directed to the North Central region where preservation in its natural state is essential.

Heart Lake is one of several alpine beauties locked
in deep glacier-carved pockets near timberline in
the Alpine Lakes area.

Seasonal transition in the Alpine Lakes: Here in
midsummer, deep winter snow still lingers as a
lakelet begins shedding its blanket and glacier lilies
follow the snowline as it recedes up the mountain
slopes.

Enchantment Lakes on the glacier-scoured granite plateau near the crest of the Stuart Range: The spectacular granite peaks surrounding the lakes belie the fragile beauty of the area, which must be treated with reverence to preserve the sparse stand of larch trees. Larch reach their height of beauty when their needles turn to gold in the autumn.

Colchuk Lake nestles at the base of 3,000-foot granite cliffs of the Stuart Range. The lake is dyed turquoise by glacial silt.

Paint brush, cinquefoil and moss hug the sides of
a tiny rivulet as it gains momentum for its descent
of the mountains.

A deer shows more curiosity than alarm when she
discovers a strange visitor in her home.

Hundreds of species of Fungus and Mushrooms grow from decaying wood and from rich soil of the forest floor. They add their bit of color and interest to the woodlands. Some wild mushrooms are a gourmet's delight but others like Amanita muscaria, upper right, are poisonous.

Devils club foliage spreads like umbrellas over the forest floor but fails to prevent heavy rainfall from nourishing abundant plantlife that thrives in the moist climate of the western foothills.

A mosaic carpet of autumn foliage creates a colorful setting for an unnamed lake and the aptly named Jade Lake which owes its color to dissolved glacial silt.

Cinquefoil and Saxifrage.

Sparkling raindrops are held like jewels in the clasp
of Lupine foliage.

Winter snow temporarily heals scars of civilization
of Snoqualmie Summit and begins a season of winter sports.

Doubtful Lake nestled in an old glacial circ of
Sahale Mountain is a popular camping spot for
hikers and climbers in North Cascades National
Park.

Nothing is more refreshing than the clear, sweet
water of a swift stream beside a wilderness trail.

Forest giants of the Suiattle River Valley in the
Glacier Peak Wilderness include cedar, Douglas
fir, spruce and hemlock.

A long pack string traverses the lush green meadows of McAlester Pass.

A whistling marmot watches with curiosity the invasion of his wilderness domain.

Mt. Shuksan in North Cascades National Park is proclaimed by photographers to be the most photogenic mountain in America. It certainly is one of the most challenging for mountaineers. Highwood Lake in the foreground is in the Mt. Baker National Forest.

Rugged peaks scrape the clouds above Diablo Lake
in the Ross Lake National Recreational area.
Diablo and Ross Lakes were created by power
dams on the Skagit River.

The clear waters of Buck Creek ramble down a
boulder-strewn forest corridor.

A canopy of cedar bows with their needles glowing
in brilliant sunlight, reach out across a swift flowing
stream.

The imposing beauty of Chewawa Mountain dominates Lyman Lakes in the Glacier Peak Wilderness.

An autumn storm abates to reveal a mystical scene of new snow on the crags of Bonanza Peak; a shallow pool beside Lyman Lake mirrors the beauty of the wilderness.

Drifting clouds pause to hover in the valley of the
Suiattle as stormy weather envelops surrounding
mountains.

The atmosphere has been washed clean by the passing of a summer storm, unveiling the grandeur of Image Lake and snow peaks of Glacier Peak Wilderness.

Thundering cataracts and waterfalls too numerous to count dash over granite cliffs at the head of a great glacier circ below Mt. Logan and Park Creek Pass in the North Cascade National Park.

Alpine wildflowers flourish in unbelievable variety and abundance in open meadows on the crest of Liberty Cap in the Glacier Peak Wilderness.

A party of mountaineers descending a snowfield of Mt. Logan enjoy a sweeping view of Goode Mountain, one of the most challenging peaks in North Cascades National Park.

Summer storm clouds melt away at sunset to unveil
a view of Glacier Peak across Image Lake.

The Pickett Range and Challenger Glacier. This is
probably the most rugged and inaccessible area in
North Cascades National Park.

Gold sparkles from larch needles in the fall on the
windswept timberline of the North Cascades.

The last light of the day silhouettes Table Mountain as a skier leaves the Austin Pass shelter in Mt. Baker National Forest.

Ski slopes are deserted as the last rays of the winter
sun bathe Mt. Shuksan's rugged crest.

An autumn snowstorm sprinkles the timberline slopes of Mt. Baker National Forest.

Mt. Baker's glacier-clad dome reaches 10,778 feet
to reflect the first light of a new day in the North
Cascades.

Photo on pages 178-179
The serrated crags and glaciers of the Ten Peak
Mountain Range rims forested slopes and valley of
the Suiattle River. The photo was taken from
Flower Dome near Buck Creek Pass in Glacier
Peak Wilderness.

The Long Adventure

When I first saw a picture of Mt. Hood in a Midwestern grade school geography book, it became something of a beacon to me as it was in reality to pioneers who first saw it as their covered wagons rolled across the sagebrush land of Eastern Oregon en route to fertile Willamette Valley farmland.

I managed to work my way West in the late 1920's and first saw the great peak from its most impressive north side when I came to the Hood River Valley as a transient apple picker in 1927. It was there that I became enamoured with the Cascades. From my little transient's shack on a hillside I could look out across the beautiful Hood River Valley orchard land to Mt. Adams, about 40 miles away in Washington. A short hike around the shoulder of the hill gave a view of the north face of Mt. Hood.

Then one night there was a heavy rainfall in the valley and the morning dawned crisp and clear to reveal Mt. Adams enrobed in its new autumn cloak of snow. Mt. Hood was a gleaming white sentinel towering high above the south end of the valley, only a few miles away. Since that morning I have never since wished to live any place other than the Northwest.

I explored the valley and surrounding foothills at every opportunity, and one Sunday I managed to force my Model T Ford up the then muddy, narrow, twisting road through the dense evergreen forests to Lost Lake. Although I did not realize it at the time, conditions could not have been more perfect for that classic view of the mountain with its new cloak of snow. It intensified my desire to stay in the Northwest and see more of this great mountain range.

Since then I have enjoyed the thrills of climbing Mt. Hood many times, summer and winter, exploring its glaciers, trails, streams and the new and improved roads surrounding it. I spent one miserable winter night in the foul-smelling, sulfur-steam filled snow caves in Mt. Hood's crater, freezing on one side and soaking wet with steam on the other.

I have climbed several other high volcanic cones as well as some rugged lower peaks. My first ascent of a major peak was Mt. Shasta in Northern California while working my way to the Northwest. I have watched from the crest of Mt. Hood as the rising sun cast a 100-mile symmetrical shadow of the peak's cone across a sea of clouds to the west. Then, as the shadow slowly shortened with the ascent of the sun in the clear sky, there was time to appreciate a magnificent panorama of space and clouds broken only by other volcanic peaks of the range reaching high into the sunlight like islands in the vast blanket of clouds enveloping the lower ridges and valleys.

Memories of other ascents, some unpleasant or arduous experiences, are still vivid: The conquest of Mt. Rainier in a windstorm so violent that the sun shining in an otherwise clear sky could barely be seen through blowing snow and ice; a climb of Mt. Adams, ordinarily a tedious ascent by the most-used south-slope route, was turned into one of the most thrilling of climbs by our decision to explore the fantastic bergshrunds and crevasses of the Klickitat Glacier just below the summit. It was from that day on that the glaciers became my goal more often than the conquest of the peaks themselves. Exploring the ever-changing crevasses and seracs of glacier ice falls is, for me, one of the most thrilling aspects of mountaineering.

As the Cascades have become more familiar to me, the trails have attracted more of my attention. My early impressions of the mountains were dominated by the peaks and vast panoramas. Now, more and more I notice the intimate details; I have become somewhat accustomed to the grandeur only to discover an ever-changing and more interesting aspect of our mountains. The trails provide an intimate association with the forest, streams, wildlife, and plant life that I formerly ignored in my enthusiasm to reach the higher mountain slopes. The trails unveil a never-ending revelation of nature that many of us overlook in our enthusiastic conquest of peaks or pursuit of other forms of recreation. One of my greatest pleasures is provided by the almost inexhaustible number of small clear-water streams. There is nothing quite like being able to dip a cup of cold, pure water for a refreshing drink during a rest stop and pausing to listen to the music of the cascading streams.

The low-elevation trails offer other thrills, such as coming upon a deer, bear or smaller forest animals. One night, a companion and I were hiking for a sunrise view from a 4,000-foot mountain above the Columbia River when the beam of my flashlight brought a cougar crashing down from a tree. It bounded away, probably as frightened as we were.

One time I was dragged from a rampaging stream in the North Cascades after I had fallen with my 50-pound pack from a very large and supposedly safe log bridge. My most immediate concern was for all the camera gear and film in the pack, and recovery on my own was almost impossible because I was lying on my back in the boulder-strewn rapids with the pack and my clothing becoming heavier by the second. Fortunately, I wasn't alone and my trail companions came to the rescue.

My visits with the Cascades have been made more enjoyable because my wife, Mira, a native Oregonian, shares my enjoyment for trail trips, and in self defense, she has become an avid and accomplished photographer. Together, we have watched the phenomenal increase in recreational and commercial use of the Cascades' resources — some good and some pathetic, to put it mildly. There are photographs in this book that can never be duplicated because of man's sometimes indiscriminate destruction of nature; on the other hand, others might never have been taken had there been no new roads and trails into formerly inaccessible areas. Consequently, I have seen a lot of the Cascades, but there is much more to see and I hope to continue my long adventure in my favorite mountains for many years to come.

Perhaps this selection of photographs will help influence the preservation of more natural beauty for coming generations. They will need the wilderness areas and parks even more than we who have the opportunity to preserve that which now exists.

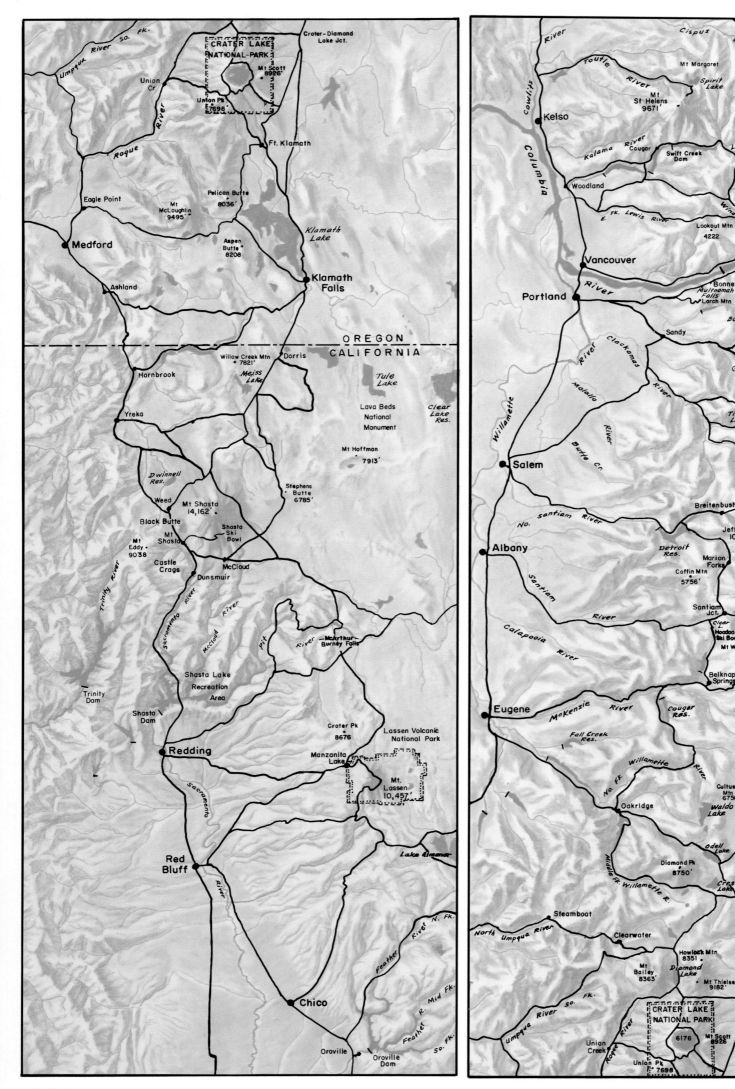

MAP 1
SOUTHERN OREGON
& NORTHERN CALIFORNIA

MAP 2
NORTHERN OREGON

180

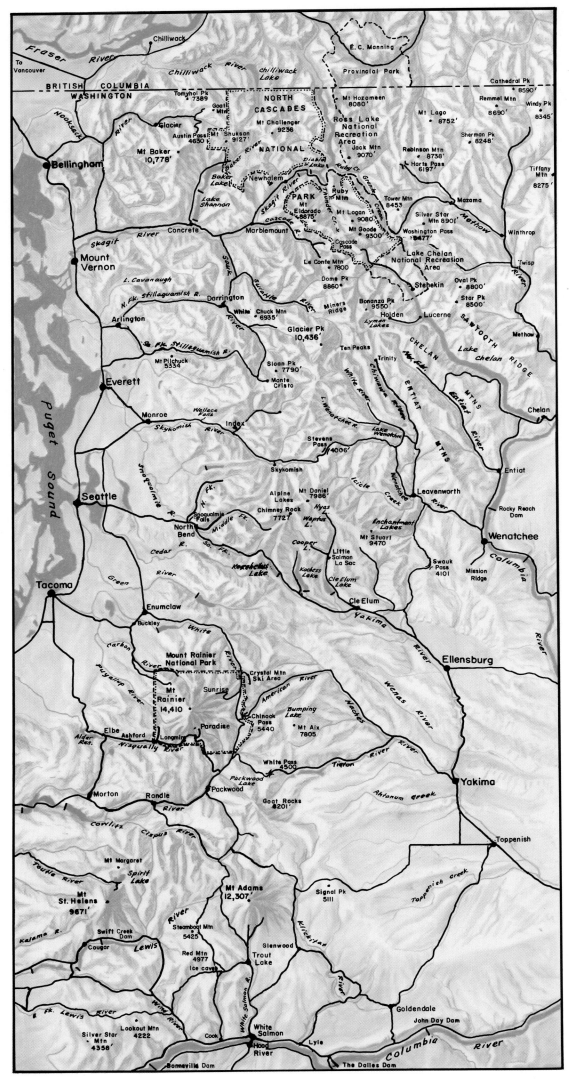

INDEX MAP

THE CASCADE RANGE

MAP 3
WASHINGTON